Irish Love & Wedding Customs

To_____

From_____

With Love

This book is dedicated to the memory of
my father-in-law, Dan McGuire,
with love and gratitude.

Irish Love & Wedding Customs

Kim McGuire

Published in 2000 by
Wolfhound Press Ltd
68 Mountjoy Square
Dublin 1, Ireland

© 2000 Kim McGuire
Illustrations © Sarah Cunningham

All rights reserved. No part of this book may be reproduced or utilised in any form or by any means digital, electronic or mechanical including photography, filming, video recording, photocopying, or by any information storage and retrieval system or shall not, by way of trade or otherwise, be lent, resold or otherwise circulated in any form of binding or cover other than that in which it is published without prior permission in writing from the publisher.

 Wolfhound Press receives financial assistance from the Arts Council/ An Chomhairle Ealaíon, Dublin.

British Library Cataloguing in Publication Data
A catalogue record for this book is available from the British Library.

ISBN 0-86327-793-4

10 9 8 7 6 5 4 3 2 1

Cover illustration: Sarah Cunningham
Cover design: Mark O'Neill
Typesetting: Wolfhound Press
Printed by Edelvives, Spain

Contents

Introduction	7
Celtic Cupid	9
Patron of Love	11
Tying the Knot	13
The Art of Kissing	15
Matchmaking Fairs	17
Courtship and Wooing	19
Divination	21
True Love	23
Unusual Proposals	25
Love Stones	27
The Claddagh	29
Bands of Love	31
The Ideal Time to Marry	33

Fixing the Day	35
Bridal Lore	37
Luck and Love for the Groom	39
The Groom's Declaration	41
Travel to the Church	43
Prayer of the Newly Weds	45
A Traditional Druidic Blessing	47
The Grushie	49
The Strawboys	51
The Wedding Cake & Recipe	53
Toasts from the Heart & Black Velvets	55
An Irish Blessing	57
Mead	59
An Anniversary Prayer & Anniversaries	61
Folk Wisdom and Sayings	63
Bibliography	64

Introduction

While writing *The Irish Wedding Book*, I was drawn to the love and marriage traditions of Ireland. At first my fascination in them was a way of learning about the history of the country without having to become immersed in its tragic past. Eventually, however, my curiosity was piqued and I was keen to know even more.

As I came to appreciate Ireland, I was moved to share my unique perspective, which I call 'the Irish in love'. Indeed, it reflects only one small aspect of the Irish nature, but it is rich and deserves to be remembered.

I hope that as you read this book you will be entertained and enlightened. There are so many ways to discover and explore history; for me, the best way has been through the heart.

Celtic Cupid

Many gods have been said to preside over affairs of the heart, but in Celtic tradition only Aengus Óg embodies love and beauty. Born of a secret union between Daghdagh, the mightiest of Irish gods, and Boann, the river goddess, he is depicted as an eternally youthful purveyor of romance. The Celts believed that his magic kisses became tiny birds and whoever heard their sweet singing would suddenly be overcome with passionate notions.

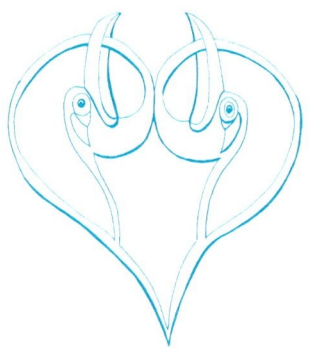

Patron of Love

February 14th is universally acknowledged as a special day for lovers, but very few people know why the holiday is of particular importance to the Irish. In the early 1900s, Pope Gregory XVI entrusted the remains of Valentine, the Catholic saint for whom the day is named, to the people of Ireland, because they had such a great devotion to the martyr at the time. In 1953, a shrine was built in Valentine's honour at Whitefriar Street Church in Dublin, and to this day his relics are venerated there.

Tying the Knot

harvest knots were once a popular gift exchanged by courting couples in rural Ireland. In the autumn, stalks of corn or strands of hay were braided into intricate patterns to create beautiful symbols of love. It is said that, whenever possible, young men left the grains on their harvest knots to symbolise future fertility and the family to come.

The Art of Kissing

Give me, my love, that billing kiss
I taught you one delicious night,
When, turning epicures in bliss,
We tried inventions of delight.

Come gently steal my lips along,
And let your lips in murmurs move,
Ah, no! — again — that kiss was wrong,
How can you be so dull, my love!

'Cease, cease!' the blushing girl replied
and in her milky arms she caught me.
'How can you thus your pupil chide:
You know 'twas in the dark you taught me!'

— 'The Kiss' by Thomas Moore

Matchmaking Fairs

Country fairs and hill assemblies were ancient celebrations once held all over Ireland for the purpose of bringing lovers together. One very old meeting-place was Lisdoonvarna, in north County Clare, where, to this day, the autumn festival is called Garland Sunday. This week-long fête, with its dances, games and song competitions, brings eligible singles from around the world together in search of a perfect match.

Courtship and Wooing

For centuries, romantic love was a luxury of the landless, while marriages between the well-to-do were always arranged. Wealthy parents protected their family name, financial security and social status by not leaving love to chance. The daughter of a prosperous farmer, for example, would never be allowed to marry a young man of poorer standing. One old Irish saying put it simply: 'When poverty comes in the door, love flies out the window.'

Divination

When beauty and charm failed to move a man in the direction of the altar, Irish lasses relied on spells, incantations and magic potions. To cast a love spell, a young woman would chant the following three times while serving him a drink:

> This is the charm I set for love, a woman's charm of love and desire:
>
> a charm of God that none can break.
>
> You for me and I for thee, and for none else:
>
> your face to mine and your head turned away from all others.

To dream of your true love, pluck a two-rooted briar on Halloween night. Make a ring of it, take it home and place it under your pillow. During the night, your true love will come to you in a dream.

True Love

I love my Love in the morning,
I love my Love at noon,
For she is bright as the lord of light,
Yet mild as Autumn's moon.

Her beauty is my bosom's sun,
Her faith my fostering shade,
And I will love my darling one
Till ever the sun shall fade....

— 'I love my Love in the morning'
by Gerald Griffin

Unusual Proposals

Love may be the soul of an Irish man but, when it comes to proposing, it is hard to know whether he is truly bashful or simply a rogue.

> 'Would you like to be buried with my people?'
>
> — Anon

> 'Would you like to hang your washing with mine?'
>
> — Anon

> 'Would you like to share my pillow?'
>
> — Anon

Love Stones

In County Antrim and on the Aran Islands there are tall stone monuments, with a single hole piercing their centre. For centuries these 'standing stones', as they were called, were thought to have magic powers. Local folklore claims that the stones bestow everlasting love on couples who clasp hands through their middle.

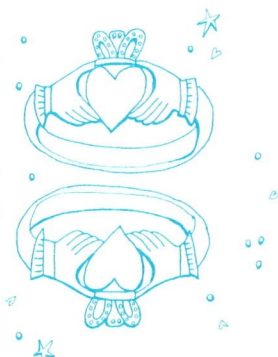

The Claddagh

For more than four hundred years, the Claddagh has been a love symbol unique to the west of Ireland. Named after an ancient Galway fishing village for where it was first designed, the Claddagh depicts two hands holding a crowned heart. For generations these rings were worn only by the people of the area and were handed down through families by a mother to the first of her daughters married.

When the Claddagh is worn on the right hand and the tip of the heart is facing upwards, it tells others that the wearer is single. Placed the same way on the left hand, it reveals that love is being considered. When worn on the left hand, with the crown turned upwards, it shows all that the wearer is married.

Bands of Love

The origins of the wedding ring may be lost forever, but it seems always to have been a symbol of the marriage contract between husband and wife. In Ireland the first known rings were made of gold, silver, bronze or wood.

The custom of writing inscriptions on the inner surface of wedding bands was introduced by the Romans and Greeks and became popular in Ireland in the sixteenth century. Some romantic Irish sentiments include:

> God above increase our love.
>
> Let love and friendship reign.
>
> I long to be made one with thee.
>
> Time shall tell I love thee well.
>
> God's blessing on thee and me.
>
> Love for love.

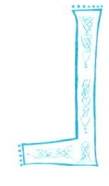

The Ideal Time to Marry

November is the time to wed, the harvest's in and it's cold in bed.

This old Irish adage led people to believe that autumn and winter were the times in which to marry. Another verse, which is popular in Ireland but is most likely English in origin, suggests that there may have been some months more lucky than others.

> Marry in September's shine,
> Your living will be rich and fine.
> If in October you do marry
> Love will come but riches tarry.
> If you wed in bleak November
> Only joy will come, remember.
> When December's showers fall fast
> Marry and true love will last.

Fixing the Day

Choosing the right day on which to marry was important to Irish brides. The ancient wisdom was that a growing moon and a flowing tide were lucky times, but some couples wanted a more specific date. Long ago, marriages were forbidden during Lent, as it was a time for doing penance. However, St Patrick's Day and Shrove Tuesday were considered the best days of the year for a wedding.

An old rhyme, most likely borrowed from the English, offered even more detailed advice about when to marry:

> Monday for health;
> Tuesday for wealth;
> Wednesday the best day of all.
> Thursday for losses;
> Friday for crosses;
> Saturday no day at all.

Bridal Lore

Green is the colour of Ireland, but it is not suitable for Irish weddings. According to legend, the colour entices mischievous fairies, who love to possess all things beautiful — especially brides. Rather than tempt the little creatures, a bride should wear something blue, as it is considered the colour of true love.

Long ago, Ulster brides always stopped by the blacksmith's forge on their wedding day to collect a horseshoe for luck. Today, to carry on the custom, a tiny horseshoe is sewn into a bridal gown or included in the bouquet.

Crossing the path of a black cat will bring good luck to a bride on her wedding day. To see a lamb or dove before the ceremony will double her good fortune.

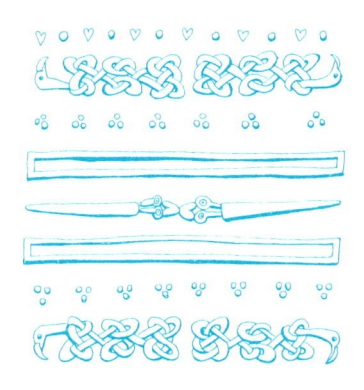

Luck and Love for the Groom

To bring good luck to his marriage, a groom will follow the custom of his ancient ancestors and grow a beard for his wedding day. Beards were once very much a part of the Irishman's appearance and no chieftain went without one.

To ensure a life of happiness, a husband should present his bride with some freshly churned butter, while standing beside a tree or a stream, and say:

> O woman, loved by me,
> mayest thou give me thy heart,
> thy soul and thy body.

For extra luck, a groom should be the first to kiss his bride after the ceremony. In Ireland this is not always easy to do, as the groomsmen usually try to beat the unsuspecting groom to this honour.

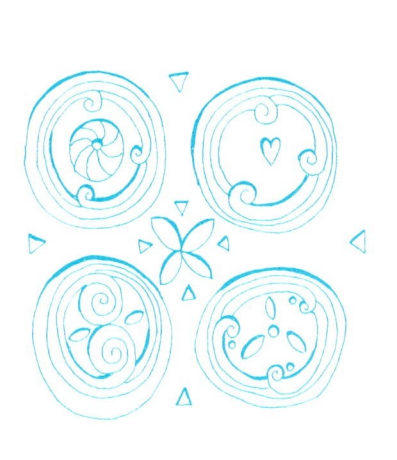

The Groom's Declaration

During the marriage ceremony, immediately following the blessing of rings, an Irish groom presents his bride with a small gift and says, 'I give you this gold and silver as a token of all I possess.' The offering, usually a newly minted coin, is symbolic of the couple's unity in marriage and the groom's willingness to share his wealth and worldly possessions. After the wedding, the gift is preserved as an heirloom and is passed from mother to eldest son on his wedding day.

Travel to the Church

In centuries past, people from the country did not believe it unlucky for the bride and groom to see each other on the morning of their wedding. Oftentimes, they would meet before the ceremony and walk the distance from home to church together in the company of family and friends.

Today this tradition is rarely practised. It is now customary for the groom and his groomsmen to make their own way to the church, for the bridesmaids to be provided with transportation by the bride's family, and for the bride and her father to arrive by limousine. The bridal car is specially decorated for the day: two white satin ribbons are secured to the window frames of the front doors and tied into a pretty bow at the centre of the hood.

Prayer of the Newly Weds

The following prayer is often recited by the bride and groom together during the marriage ceremony, immediately following the exchange of rings:

> We thank you, Lord, and we praise you for bringing us to this happy day. You have given us to each other. Now, together, we give ourselves to you. We ask you, Lord: make us one in your love, keep us one in your peace. Protect our marriage. Bless our home. Make us gentle. Keep us faithful. And, when life is over, unite us again where parting is no more, in the kingdom of your love. There we will praise you in the happiness and peace of our eternal home. Amen.

A Traditional Druidic Blessing

We swear by peace and love to stand,
Heart to heart and hand to hand.
Hark, O Spirit, and hear us now,
Confirming this our Sacred Vow.

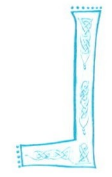

The Grushie

Among prosperous families it was, and in some places still is, customary for the groom to toss a handful of coins into the air to a crowd of guests gathered on the steps of the church. The 'grushie', as this custom is called, is performed after the ceremony and is believed to bring good fortune to the groom and his bride.

The Strawboys

One of the oldest features of a traditional Irish wedding reception is the visitation of the strawboys. Young men, acting out the role of uninvited guests, disguise themselves in masks, hats and coats of straw and lay claim to the privilege of dancing with the bride. They are warmly received and given plenty of food and drink. In return, they entertain guests with their singing and dancing.

The strawboys are always made to feel welcome, and their absence from a wedding is a bad omen. After dancing with the bride, the leader of the group places a crown of straw on her head and presents her with a horseshoe for good luck.

A Wedding Cake Recipe

Irish wedding cakes are lush fruit confections wrapped in marzipan and draped with royal icing. The following recipe makes one small layer and can be made three months ahead.

340g/12 oz (3 cups) self-raising flour
170g/6 oz (5 tbsp) margarine
560g/1¼ lb (2¼ cups) chopped dried fruit
110g/4 oz (1¼ cup) chopped peel
170g/6 oz (¾ cup) sugar
1 tsp ground cinnamon/clove/nutmeg

¼ tsp salt
3 well-beaten eggs
5 tbsp brandy
2 tbsp milk

Preheat oven to 160°C/325°F. Grease and line an 8–9 inch round, springform clip tin with greaseproof (wax) paper. Mix all ingredients until evenly blended. Spoon batter into tin. Bake for 1 hour. Test cake with skewer; if it comes out clean, the cake is done. Let cool. Turn out, wrap and store until ready to decorate.

The Wedding Cake

Cakes have been a familiar symbol of weddings since Roman times. At an Irish wedding, guests are given small white boxes containing slices of cake to take home as favours. Extra slices are also boxed and sent to guests who cannot attend the ceremony.

It was once believed that slipping a piece of bridal cake under your pillow would bring about a dream of your future spouse.

Newly weds save the top layer of their wedding cake for the christening of their first baby. After the wedding, a glass of whiskey is poured on top of the cake and the cake is then carefully wrapped and stored in a cool place. On the day of the baby's christening, the cake is sliced into tiny pieces and given as a special treat to guests.

Black Velvets

Champagne may be the traditional drink of choice for toasting a couple's health and happiness, but an Irish couple should be toasted with a Black Velvet. To make this deliciously smooth drink, fill a flute glass halfway with champagne and top it up with Guinness.

Toasts from the Heart

'May your fire never go out.'

— Anon

'May you climb the road of success
and never meet a friend coming down.'

— Anon

'Let your anger set with the sun
and not rise with it again.'

— Thomas Moore

'May you have many children and may they grow
as mature in taste, healthy in colour
and as sought after as the contents of this glass.'

— Anon

An Irish Blessing

May the road rise to meet you,
And the wind be always at your back.
May the sun shine warm upon your face,
The rain fall soft upon your fields.
And, until we meet again,
May the Lord hold you in the palm of His hand.

Mead

The Irish for honeymoon, 'mí na meala' — literally, 'month of honey' — dates back to the fifth century, when couples drank a honeyed wine, called mead, for one full cycle of the moon. Originally brewed by Irish monks for medicinal purposes, it became a popular wedding drink because of its supposed ability to enhance fertility. Today, mead is produced at a small winery in County Clare and is exported around the world.

Wedding Anniversaries

First	Paper	Thirteenth	Lace
Second	Cotton	Fourteenth	Ivory
Third	Leather	Fifteenth	Crystal
Fourth	Flowers	Twentieth	China
Fifth	Wood	Twenty-fifth	Silver
Sixth	Candy	Thirtieth	Pearl
Seventh	Copper	Thirty-fifth	Coral
Eighth	Bronze	Fortieth	Ruby
Ninth	Pottery	Forty-fifth	Sapphire
Tenth	Tin	Fiftieth	Gold
Eleventh	Steel	Fifty-fifth	Emerald
Twelfth	Linen	Sixtieth	Diamond

An Anniversary Prayer

May your mornings bring joy and your evenings bring peace.
May your troubles grow few as your blessings increase.
May the saddest day of your future
be no worse than the happiest day of your past.
May your hands be forever clasped in friendship
and your hearts joined forever in love.
Your lives are very special,
God has touched you in many ways.
May his blessings rest upon you
and fill all your coming days.

Folk Wisdom and Sayings

Francis Bacon wrote that 'the genius, wit and spirit of a nation are discovered in its proverbs'. When it comes to Irish folk wisdom and sayings, no truer words could be said.

Court abroad but marry at home.

A light heart lives long.

Happy is the bride the rain falls softly on.

Your feet will bring you where your heart is.

It's a lonesome washing without a man's shirt in it.

Marriage has many pains, but celibacy has no pleasures.

Woe to him who does not heed a good wife's counsel.

Bibliography

Baker, Margaret, *Wedding Customs and Folklore*, 1977.
Brown, Raymond L., *A Book of Superstitions*, 1970.
Cosgrove, Art, *Marriage in Ireland*, 1985.
Danaher, Kevin, *The Year in Ireland*, 1972.
Day, Robert, 'Poesy Rings', *Royal Historical & Archaeological Society Journal*, 1883.
Evans, E.E., *Irish Folk Ways*, 1957.
Foster, Jeanne C., *Ulster Folklore*, 1951.
Hutchinson, Rev. H.N., *Marriage Customs in Many Lands*, 1897.
Joyce, Cecily, *Claddagh Ring Story*, 1990.
Lawrence, Robert M., *The Magic of the Horseshoe*, 1898.
McCann, Sean, *The Irish in Love*, 1972.
Mooney, James, *The Holiday Customs of Ireland*, 1889.
Powers, Patrick C., *Sex and Marriage in Ancient Ireland*, 1976.
Tynan, Katharine, *Irish Love Songs*, 1892.
Wilde, Lady Jane, *Ancient Cures, Charms and Usages in Ireland*, 1890.